CHARLOTTE HORNETS

RICHARD RAMBECK

COVER AND TITLE PAGE PHOTOS BY MATT MAHURIN

CREATIVE EDUCATION

Published by Creative Education, Inc.

123 S. Broad Street, Mankato, Minnesota 56001 USA

Art Director, Rita Marshall
Cover and title page photography by Matt Mahurin
Book design by Rita Marshall

Photos by: Allsport; Mel Bailey; Bettmann Archive;
Brian Drake; Duomo; Focus On Sports; FPG; Tim
O'Dell; South Florida Images Inc.; Spectra-Action;
Sportschrome; Sports Photo Masters, Inc.; SportsLight:
Brian Drake, Long Photography; Wide World Photos.

Library of Congress Cataloging-in-Publication Data

Rambeck, Richard.

Charlotte Hornets / Richard Rambeck.

Summary: A history of the NBA expansion team that
began playing in Charlotte, North Carolina, during the
1988-89 season.

ISBN 0-88682-559-8

1. Charlotte Hornets (Basketball team)—History—
Juvenile literature. [1. Charlotte Hornets (Basketball
team)—History. 2. Basketball—History.] I. Title.
GV885.52.C4R36 1992   92-3165
796.323'64'0975676—dc20   CIP

CHARLOTTE: HOME OF THE HORNETS

In 1799, miners in Charlotte, North Carolina, made a startling discovery. They struck gold—the first major find of that precious metal in the United States. The miners' lucky strike attracted national attention to their village, which had been founded by Scottish and Irish immigrants in the 1740s and named after Britain's Queen Charlotte.

Since then, the small village of Charlotte has grown into North Carolina's largest city, as well as one of the largest metropolitan areas in the southeastern United States. Located in the south central part of the state, Charlotte is a center for the cotton, tobacco, and textile industries. It is also the headquarters of two large banks that have played an important part in the growth of the region.

An original Hornet, forward Kelly Tripucka.

In May 1987, more than 50,000 fans turned out for a parade to celebrate the NBA's arrival in Charlotte.

But Charlotte is known for more than its rich history and growing industries. It is also known for its tradition of sports—particularly college sports. Basketball is king in North Carolina. Powerful college programs have been built at four colleges in the state: the University of North Carolina, North Carolina State, Duke, and Wake Forest. All of these schools are members of the Atlantic Coast Conference, which usually holds its postseason tournament in Charlotte. The ACC tournaments the city hosted over the years gave Charlotte residents a taste of great basketball, but many local sports fans hoped for more. They longed to see pro hoops played in their state. Their dream came true in 1988.

SHINN SHOOTS FOR THE MOON: PRO BASKETBALL

The man most responsible for bringing professional basketball to North Carolina was a Charlotte businessman named George Shinn. Shinn was certain that, because of North Carolina's great basketball tradition and Charlotte's growing population, the city would be a great place for a professional franchise.

Others told Shinn he was crazy. "Charlotte will never get a professional team of any kind," they said. "The city and surrounding communities aren't big enough to support a pro franchise."

Shinn didn't listen. He knew that the National Basketball Association was planning to expand in the late 1980s. Shinn, who had previously tried unsuccessfully to bring pro football to North Carolina, vowed to land an NBA expansion team for Charlotte.

Robert Reid: a shooting star.

In October 1989, George Shinn organized a Hornets exhibition game that raised $150,000 for a homeless shelter.

If anyone could handle the challenge, it was George Shinn. He had been beating the odds all his life. Shinn was born in Kannapolis, North Carolina, about 25 miles from Charlotte. His father died when George was eight, and the family had a hard time making ends meet. Shinn didn't do well in school, but he didn't let this hold him back. He had natural ability as a businessman, and a way of convincing people the impossible could be done.

Shinn started out by purchasing a string of failing business schools and turning them into successful enterprises. He also made a lot of money in real estate and car dealerships.

Now he was ready for a new challenge. Shinn convinced several other local businessmen to help him try to get an NBA expansion franchise for Charlotte. He formed Charlotte's NBA Executive Advisory Committee, which held a contest to name the team in November 1986. The name that was eventually chosen was "Hornets."

Charlotte now had a name for its team, but would it ever receive a franchise? Many of the leaders of the NBA doubted that pro basketball could succeed in college basketball-crazy North Carolina. "If there were eight cities being seriously considered for expansion, Charlotte probably ranked ninth," said one NBA official. But Shinn was determined.

He showed the NBA executives plans for a new arena, which was about to be completed—an arena that, with almost 24,000 seats, would be one of the largest in the league. Shinn also told the NBA that the Charlotte Hornets had already sold 8,500 season tickets for a team that might never even have a season. NBA officials, obviously impressed, awarded Charlotte an expansion franchise in April 1987. The team would begin playing in the 1988-89 season.

FINDING A COACH, BUILDING A TEAM

At 59 years of age, "veteran" Dick Harter was the league's oldest coach in 1988-89.

George Shinn had seemingly done the impossible in bringing an NBA franchise to Charlotte, but the job of establishing a team was just beginning. The club needed a coach and players. The Hornets hired Dick Harter to lead the team on the court. Harter had been an outstanding college coach as well as an assistant with several NBA teams. He was a hard-nosed type who preached hustle and defense. He ate, drank, and slept basketball—that is, when he could sleep. "The day I can sleep after a loss is the day I'll quit coaching," Harter claimed. "I'll do the same thing [quit] the day I bring the loss the night before to practice the next day. It just isn't professional."

Harter was prepared to face many sleepless nights, for he knew the Hornets wouldn't be winners at first. The team's initial roster would be composed of players obtained from two main sources: other clubs in the league and the college draft. Harter couldn't expect a team of castoffs from other clubs and young fresh-out-of-college players to compete with the best teams in the NBA. But he set out to build the best team he could.

First, the Hornets and the Miami Heat—the other new team added to the league in 1988-89—took part in a special veteran player draft. Each established NBA club was

Young star Kendall Gill.

A crowd favorite, the talented Muggsy Bogues.

Leading scorer Kelly Tripucka topped the 40-point mark three times in 1988-89.

allowed to protect eight players from being drafted by the expansion teams. The remaining players were available to the Hornets and the Heat. The Hornets acquired high-scoring forward Kelly Tripucka from the Utah Jazz, steady guard Robert Reid from the Houston Rockets, rugged forward Kurt Rambis from the Los Angeles Lakers, big guard Dell Curry from the Cleveland Cavaliers, and tiny Tyrone "Muggsy" Bogues from the Washington Bullets.

"TOO SMALL" BOGUES STANDS TALL

The most popular player among the new Hornets was its smallest star—Muggsy Bogues. Bogues, who had played his college ball in North Carolina at Wake Forest, was only 5-foot-3, but he drove opponents crazy with his quickness and ball-handling skills. Bogues had been selected by Washington in the first round of the 1987 college draft. Many experts were surprised when, a year later, the Bullets did not protect him in the expansion draft. The Hornets jumped at the chance to take Bogues, who became a favorite of George Shinn. "Muggsy was my pick. I wanted somebody I could see eye-to-eye with," said Shinn, who was only 5-foot-7 himself.

Bogues had Shinn's respect, but others, including opponents, looked down on the little guard and dismissed his abilities. Los Angeles Laker guard Michael Cooper said guarding Bogues was like "playing one-on-one with my six-year-old." That kind of attitude made Bogues work harder. "Everyone's been telling me I was too short ever since I started playing ball," Bogues complained. "But when we put our sneakers on and get out on the floor, my heart makes me as good as anyone else."

Kurt Rambis, at only 6-foot-8, was the NBA's 15th-best rebounder in 1988-89.

REX CHAPMAN RACKS UP THE POINTS

While some may have questioned Bogues' ability, nobody doubted the skills of Charlotte's first-ever choice in the college draft. Picking eighth in the 1988 draft, the Hornets selected 6-foot-5 guard Rex Chapman from the University of Kentucky. Chapman was a marvelous shooter with incredible jumping ability.

The son of a basketball coach, Chapman grew up in Kentucky, a state as basketball-crazy as North Carolina. When he graduated from high school, Chapman was considered one of the top young players in the country. He enrolled at the University of Kentucky, a college with a

Rex Chapman sank at least one three-pointer in 14 straight games during his rookie season.

long history of great teams and players. One writer for *Sports Illustrated* predicted Chapman would lead the Wildcats to a couple of NCAA titles before he graduated. "It's flattering," Chapman said, "but if I start listening to that stuff, I won't get any better." After playing only two seasons at Kentucky, Chapman decided that the best way to get better was to take on the best players in the world—in the NBA. So he entered his name in the college draft and soon became Charlotte's number-one pick.

During his first few months in Charlotte, Chapman had some trouble adjusting to the pro game. It was much more physical than college ball, and the slender Chapman took a beating. Early in the season, veteran teammate Kurt Rambis took the young guard aside. "They're coming at you, Rex, because you're a rookie," Rambis explained patiently. "You've got to take it personally, or it's going to keep happening. Stay low, lean into them, don't worry about getting beat. It happens, but make it a pain for anyone to go after you."

Chapman listened and learned. He became tougher on the court. In fact, he even grew a beard to make himself look meaner, which didn't sit too well with George Shinn. "Son," Shinn said to Chapman in a fatherly tone, "I just wanted you to know my 11-year-old daughter thinks the world of you. But that stuff you're growing on your face is just spoiling the All-American image. I wouldn't want you to do anything for her to fall out of love with you." After hearing Shinn's words, Chapman shaved off the beard.

Chapman and the Hornets had some rough going at the beginning of their initial season. In the team's first game, the Hornets fell to Cleveland on the road, 133-93. Four days

Charlotte's first college draft pick, Rex Chapman.

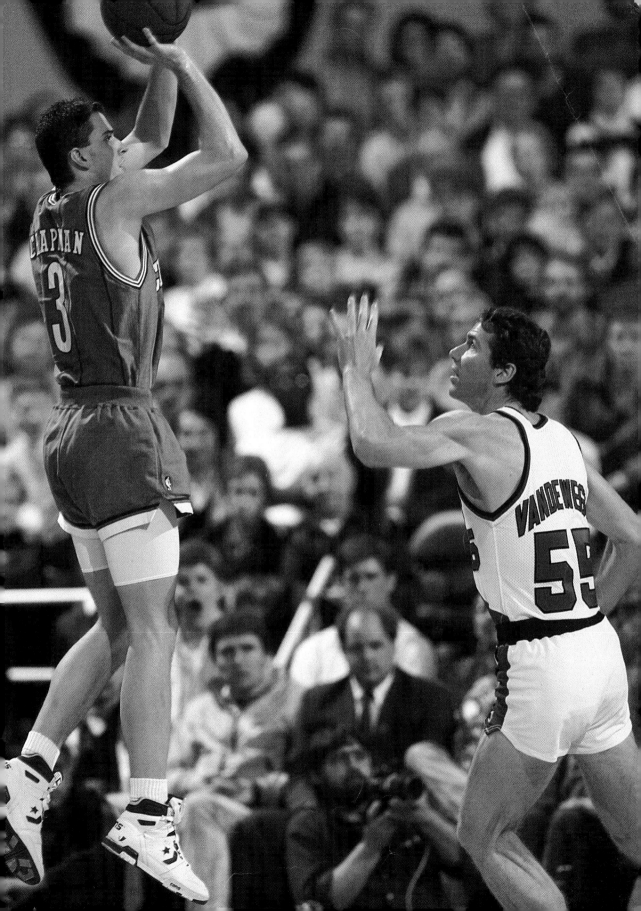

later, however, Charlotte registered its first victory. On November 8, 1988, the night George Bush was elected president of the United States, the Hornets defeated the Los Angeles Clippers, 117-105, in front of almost 24,000 screaming fans at home.

Three weeks after their first victory, the Hornets beat Miami, the other expansion team, 99-84. The game was played in Charlotte, and the Hornets fans helped turn up the temperature on the Miami Heat. "Charlotte's crowd is more like a college crowd," said Miami center Rony Seikaly. "It's a great help for the Hornets, like a sixth man for them."

Charlotte's biggest victory in its first season came two days before Christmas against the Chicago Bulls. The game was a homecoming for Chicago star Michael Jordan, who

Kenny Gattison joined Charlotte in 1989.

In one of the first games in his rookie season, J.R. Reid scored 25 points and grabbed 20 rebounds.

had been a standout at the University of North Carolina. A sellout crowd warmly welcomed Jordan, but the fans cheered even louder for their team. The game, which was on national television, was close all the way to the end.

With seconds left, Kurt Rambis rebounded a missed Charlotte shot. With two Bulls draped all over him, Rambis muscled in for the winning shot, which dropped as the buzzer sounded. The crowd poured onto the court in celebration of the most exciting moment in the history of the young franchise. "It's very difficult to play against Michael Jordan," Charlotte coach Dick Harter said of the Chicago star, who had scored 40 points. "But it's a Merry Christmas game for the people of Charlotte, and they deserve it."

Charlotte fans had 20 victories to cheer about during the 1988-89 season. They applauded strong performances from veterans Kelly Tripucka, who led the team in scoring with a 22.6 average, and Robert Reid, who averaged almost 15 points per game. Several of the club's youngsters also became crowd favorites. Rex Chapman was second in scoring with a 16.9 average, and Muggsy Bogues topped the Hornets in assists and all-around hustle.

But the real stars of the 1988-89 season were the Charlotte fans themselves. The first-year franchise led the league in attendance with an average of 23,172 per game. In other words, the club sold out every game played in the Charlotte Coliseum that first year. The team's overall attendance was the second highest single-season total in the history of the NBA. The Hornets might not have won many games on the court, but the franchise won over all the skeptics who said the North Carolina city would never support an NBA team.

During the 1989-90 season, Dell Curry topped the Hornets in three-pointers taken (147) and made (52).

HORNETS DRAFT A LOCAL HERO

After the end of their first season, the Hornets faced a tough decision in the 1989 NBA draft. Picking fifth in the draft, Charlotte had an opportunity to take any one of several top college stars. But George Shinn, the North Carolina native, knew whom he wanted: J.R. Reid, a 6-foot-9, 230-pound center who had been a star for the University of North Carolina. Reid combined strength with a soft shooting touch. He also was remarkably quick for a man his size.

By taking Reid, the Hornets added muscle to their front line. They added more strength in the middle of the season. On New Year's Eve, Charlotte sent veteran forward Kurt

The Hammer—Armon Gilliam.

Rambis to the Phoenix Suns for power forward Armon Gilliam. Nicknamed "the Hammer," the well-muscled Gilliam had a reputation as a ferocious rebounder.

In college at the University of Nevada-Las Vegas, Gilliam had led the Runnin' Rebels to the NCAA Final Four in 1987. The Rebels were a fast-breaking, three-point-shooting team that had little inside muscle except for Gilliam. One television broadcaster described UNLV's style of play as "you guys [the guards] shoot the ball, and Armon, you go get it if the ball doesn't go in."

Gilliam, who had been the second pick overall in the 1987 college draft, never really fit in with the Suns. He welcomed the trade to the Hornets. The Hammer wound up leading Charlotte in both scoring and rebounding during the 1989-90 season. He averaged 18.8 points and 8.8 rebounds per game for the Hornets.

Armon Gilliam led the 1989-90 Hornets in rebounds per game with an 8.8 average.

Despite Gilliam's help, the Hornets actually won one less game in 1989-90 than they had in 1988-89. Charlotte finished its second season with a 19-63 record. Team officials, upset that the club wasn't improving, fired Dick Harter in the middle of the 1989-90 season. Many of the players weren't happy with Harter's defense-oriented game. Gene Littles, who had been Charlotte's personnel director and an assistant coach, was named temporary head coach in January 1990. The Hornets, especially Rex Chapman, liked Littles and vowed to improve for him.

Having Littles as their leader may have made the players happier, but the new coach couldn't solve the club's outside shooting problem or overcome the lack of a true center on the team. To make matters worse, Chapman was injured and missed almost one-third of the season. Although the Hornets struggled, the team still got solid performances

Left to right: Mike Gminski, Gene Littles, Johnny Newman, Dell Curry.

from guard Dell Curry, who tossed in 16 points a contest; J.R. Reid, who averaged 11.1 points and 8.4 rebounds; and Tyrone Bogues, who dished out 10.7 assists per game, fourth best in the league. Reid was named to the league's All-Rookie second team.

At the end of the season, the Hornets announced that Littles would be the permanent head coach, which was welcome news to several of the players. To make Littles' job easier, the Hornets added two key players before the 1990-91 season. They used their first-round pick in the college draft to take Kendall Gill, a silky-smooth 6-foot-6 guard from the University of Illinois. In addition, Charlotte made a bold move by offering free-agent forward Johnny Newman a four-year contract worth $5 million. Newman was just the kind of player Charlotte needed: an excellent scorer who could hit the outside shot or make a quick move to the basket. The New York Knicks, the team Newman had played with for three years, decided not to match Charlotte's contract offer. Newman became a Hornet and moved right into the starting lineup.

While Newman moved in, Armon Gilliam departed. He was traded early in the 1990-91 season to Philadelphia for veteran center Mike Gminski. The Hornets were counting on Gminski to be a steadying influence on the team's many young players. In addition, with Gminski on the team, J.R. Reid could move to his natural position: power forward. Gminski lived up to expectations. He provided leadership for the Hornets and plenty of muscle. He wound up leading the team in rebounding, while fellow newcomer Newman was Charlotte's top scorer with a 16.9 average. Rookie Kendall Gill also became an instant star in Charlotte. He

In his first season in Charlotte, Johnny Newman scored 20 or more points in 30 games.

The young squad celebrates a victory (pages 26-27).

averaged 11 points a game and was named to the 1991 NBA All-Rookie first team.

Newman, Gminski, Gill, and others helped Charlotte make several positive strides during the 1990-91 season. The Hornets finished with a 26-56 record, an improvement of seven games over the previous year.

In January 1990, Mike Gminski scored the 10,000th point of his career.

After the season, Littles resigned as coach to join the team's front office staff and was replaced by Allan Bristow, who had been Charlotte's vice president of basketball operations. "He is very knowledgeable about the game," Littles said of Bristow, "and has a great eye for talent."

Bristow would get a chance to show off that eye for talent during the 1991 college draft. The Hornets were part of the NBA's draft lottery, which determines which team gets first pick. In the lottery, the names of the 11 teams that didn't make the playoffs the previous season are placed in a hat. The last name drawn gets the first pick. In this case, Charlotte was very glad to be last.

LARRY JOHNSON: A REBEL WITH A CAUSE

Winning the draft lottery allowed the Hornets to take any player they wanted. Bristow already knew who his top choice would be—a 6-foot-5, 250-pound monster of a forward from the University of Nevada-Las Vegas named Larry Johnson. During his junior year, Johnson had led the Runnin' Rebels to the 1990 NCAA title. Many thought he would then decide to skip his senior year and turn pro, but Johnson stayed in school and helped UNLV make the Final Four again in 1991. He was named NCAA Player of the Year after leading the Rebels to a 34-1 record.

Larry Johnson was a near-unanimous choice for NBA Rookie of the Year in 1992.

Johnson is not a huge man by NBA standards. Because of his great strength, however, he has always played bigger than his size and believes he can be an inside force for the Hornets. "I've been playing power forward all my life," Johnson explained. "I'd like to look at myself as somewhere between a Charles Barkley–Karl Malone type. Of course, I'm not at their level yet. But hopefully, with a couple of years in the league and some hard work, I will be… I think I can do for Charlotte what I did for Vegas."

Coach Bristow believes the powerful Johnson will be the cornerstone of a team that already possesses the speed and athletic abilities of such young stars as Johnny Newman, J.R. Reid, Kendall Gill, Dell Curry, Tyrone Bogues, and Tom Hammonds (who was acquired from the Washington Bullets in a trade for Rex Chapman midway

The powerful J.R. Reid.

NBA star Larry Johnson.

Kendall Gill's 1,622 points in 1991-92 established a new Hornets record.

through the 1991-92 season). Bristow plans to blend the Hornets' quickness with a new emphasis on defense and inside power. In the past, Charlotte has relied too much on its outside game. If all goes according to plan, Newman and Reid, both of whom like to drive to the basket, will blossom under the new system. Bristow knows his club has some distance to go before it becomes a title contender. But the ingredients are there: the inside strength of Johnson, Gminski, Hammonds, and Reid; the outside shooting and scoring talents of Curry and Newman; and the leadership and ball-handling skills of Gill and Bogues. The Hornets will only get better with experience, and will continue to thrive in a city the so-called experts said could never support professional basketball.

Charlotte may not be America's largest or richest city, but it does have a history of good luck. Three hundred years ago, the luck came in the form of gold. Now, the Charlotte Hornets are aiming to mine a little gold in the NBA.